Dear Parent:
Your child's love of reading starts here!

Every child learns to read in a different way and at his or her own speed. Some go back and forth between reading levels and read favorite books again and again. Others read through each level in order. You can help your young reader improve and become more confident by encouraging his or her own interests and abilities. From books your child reads with you to the first books he or she reads alone, there are I Can Read Books for every stage of reading:

SHARED READING
Basic language, word repetition, and whimsical illustrations, ideal for sharing with your emergent reader

BEGINNING READING
Short sentences, familiar words, and simple concepts for children eager to read on their own

READING WITH HELP
Engaging stories, longer sentences, and language play for developing readers

READING ALONE
Complex plots, challenging vocabulary, and high-interest topics for the independent reader

ADVANCED READING
Short paragraphs, chapters, and exciting themes for the perfect bridge to chapter books

I Can Read Books have introduced children to the joy of reading since 1957. Featuring award-winning authors and illustrators and a fabulous cast of beloved characters, I Can Read Books set the standard for beginning readers.

A lifetime of discovery begins with the magical words **"I Can Read!"**

Visit www.icanread.com for information
on enriching your child's reading experience.

I Can Read!

BEGINNING READING

1

Pinkalicious®

Soccer Star

For Leigha,
my shining star!
—V.K.

The author gratefully acknowledges
the artistic and editorial contributions
of Daniel Griffo and Susan Hill.

I Can Read Book® is a trademark of HarperCollins Publishers.

Pinkalicious: Soccer Star
Copyright © 2012 by Victoria Kann

PINKALICIOUS and all related logos and characters
are trademarks of Victoria Kann. Used with permission.

Based on the HarperCollins book *Pinkalicious* written by
Victoria Kann and Elizabeth Kann, illustrated by Victoria Kann
All rights reserved. Manufactured in China.
No part of this book may be used or reproduced in any manner whatsoever without
written permission except in the case of brief quotations embodied in critical articles and reviews.
For information address HarperCollins Children's Books, a division of HarperCollins Publishers,
10 East 53rd Street, New York, NY 10022.
www.icanread.com

Library of Congress catalog card number: 2011940619
ISBN 978-0-06-198965-0 (trade bdg.)—ISBN 978-0-06-198964-3 (pbk.)

12 13 14 15 16 SCP 10 9 8 7 6 5 4 3 2 1
❖
First Edition

I Can Read!

BEGINNING 1 READING

Pinkalicious

Soccer Star

by Victoria Kann

HARPER

An Imprint of HarperCollinsPublishers

Daddy gave me a new pink soccer ball.

That pink ball inspired me

to kick and score like never before!

I couldn't wait

to play the first game of the year.

Our team is called the Pinksters.

They are the Ravens.

"Pink soccer balls are for babies,"
said Kendra.

Tiffany said, "Pink stinks."

"Play ball!" said the coach.

"Think pink!" said Rose.

But I kept hearing Tiffany say

"Pink stinks."

"I'll show her pink does not stink,"

I said to Rose.

The ball came to me.

I kicked it.

It went too short.

Next the ball went too long.

Then it went crazy.

Oops!

I kicked the ball to Tiffany

by mistake.

She scored a goal.

The score was one for them,
zero for the Pinksters.

Rose scored a goal.

"Good job, Rose!" I said.

The score was tied.

One for them, one for us,

and two minutes left to play.

Then Kendra kicked the ball.

The ball sailed up high.

I heard *Pink stinks*

inside my head.

I had to get that ball!

As I ran to the ball,

Goldilicious galloped toward me.

She scooped me up on her back.

We left the park far below.

We flew across the sky.

We saw girls playing soccer
all over the world!

We flew to the pink sands of Egypt.

I made a great pass!

I did a corner kick to Spain.

"*¡Pensar en rosa!*" a girl said to me.

That's "Think pink!" in Spanish.

Cherry blossoms bloomed in China.

The girls cheered "Think pink!"

in Chinese.

"Shi fĕnhóng!"

By the time we got to Italy,

I forgot all about mean old Tiffany.

"Goldilicious, let's get back

to the game," I said.

"I've learned so much.

I think I know what to do now."

I ran.

I got the ball.

I took aim and I kicked.

I did it!

I scored!

The Pinksters won.

"Wow, good job!" said Kendra.

"Pink?" said Tiffany.

"It doesn't stink."

"Three cheers for Pinkalicious!"
said Rose.
I cheered, too.

Three cheers for
pink soccer players
everywhere!